Washington
impressions

photography by Fred Pflughoft and Gordon and Cathie Sullivan

FARCOUNTRY
PRESS

ISBN 10: 1-56037-214-1
ISBN 13: 978-1-56037-214-1
Photographs © 2002 by Fred Pflughoft and Gordon and Cathie Sullivan as indicated
© 2002 Farcountry Press

Created, produced, and designed in the United States.
Printed in Korea

12 11 10 09 08   3 4 5 6 7

Above: Roosevelt Beach on the Pacific Ocean. GORDON & CATHIE SULLIVAN

Facing page: North Head Lighthouse in Fort Canby State Park. GORDON & KATHIE SULLIVAN

Title page: Alpenglow paints Mount Rainier. GORDON & CATHIE SULLIVAN

Front cover: Mount Shuksan rises above Picture Lake in Mount Baker Snoqualmie National Forest. GORDON & CATHIE SULLIVAN

Back cover: West Sound Marina, Orcas Island. FRED PFLUGHOFT

Above: Lower Lewis Falls, Gifford Pinchot National Forest. GORDON & CATHIE SULLIVAN

Facing page: Lupine in Olympic National Park. GORDON & CATHIE SULLIVAN

Above: The Tatoosh Range. FRED PFLUGHOFT

Facing page: Chilly day on the Chewuch River near Winthrop. GORDON & CATHIE SULLIVAN

Left: Edith Creek
near Paradise,
Rainier National
Park. FRED PFLUGHOFT

Facing page:
Homestead barn
in Conboy Lake
National Wildlife
Refuge.

GORDON & CATHIE
SULLIVAN

Long Beach and the Pacific
at sunset. FRED PFLUGHOFT

Left: In Skagit County.
GORDON & CATHIE SULLIVAN

Facing page: Azurite Peak and Ridge on the Pacific Coast Scenic Trail near Harts Pass.
GORDON & CATHIE SULLIVAN

Left: Paintbrush on Olympic National Park's Hurricane Ridge. FRED PFLUGHOFT

Far left: Seattle's Lake Union, sunset. FRED PFLUGHOFT

Below: Mount Rainier in Reflection Lakes.
FRED PFLUGHOFT

Above: In the Grays Harbor Marina. GORDON & CATHIE SULLIVAN

Right: Rialto Beach at La Push. GORDON & CATHIE SULLIVAN

Left: Historic barn in Washington's southeastern corner. GORDON & CATHIE SULLIVAN

Below: Winter reflections in the Wenatchee River near Leavenworth. FRED PFLUGHOFT

Facing page: Mount Shuksan. GORDON & CATHIE SULLIVAN

Right: The cascades of Nickel Creek in Mount Rainier National Park.

FRED PFLUGHOFT

Facing page: Enjoying the park's Skyline Trail.

FRED PFLUGHOFT

Above: Starfish and mussels on Rialto Beach. FRED PFLUGHOFT

Facing page: Part of Washington's commercial fishing fleet, at rest in Westport Marina. FRED PFLUGHOFT

Left: Eagle Falls on the south fork of Skykomish River.

FRED PFLUGHOFT

Facing page: Cutthroat Peak, Okanogan National Forest.

GORDON & CATHIE SULLIVAN

Summer wheatfields near
Wilbur. GORDON & CATHIE SULLIVAN

Above: Sea-kayaking the Pacific coast. GORDON & CATHIE SULLIVAN

Facing page: Looking down the Columbia River Gorge from Underwood. FRED PFLUGHOFT

Above: The morning sun colors Mount Baker snow, as seen from Artist Point. FRED PFLUGHOFT

Facing page: Reflection Lake and 14,410-foot Mount Rainier. GORDON & CATHIE SULLIVAN

Above: Enjoying the Skagit Valley's tulips. FRED PFLUGHOFT

Facing page: Spokane County Courthouse. FRED PFLUGHOFT

Above: In Grays Harbor. GORDON & CATHIE SULLIVAN

Facing page: Rock patterns in Lake Umatilla on the Columbia River, near Paterson. FRED PFLUGHOFT

Above: A whitetail deer, on the alert. FRED PFLUGHOFT

Right: Ollalie Lake in Gifford Pinchot National Forest, with Mount Adams in the background.
GORDON & KATHIE SULLIVAN

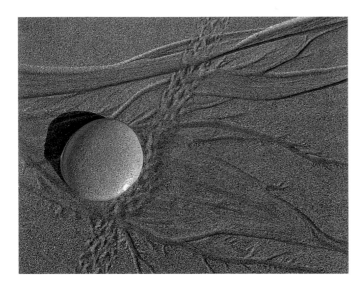

Above: Beach still life. FRED PFLUGHOFT

Right: Brown pelicans are regal when they fly. FRED PFLUGHOFT

Facing page: Seastack in the Pacific off La Push. GORDON & CATHIE SULLIVAN

Following pages: Clouds seem to be snagged atop Mount Rainier. GORDON & CATHIE SULLIVAN

Left: Parasailing over southeastern Washington verdure. GORDON & CATHIE SULLIVAN

Below: Near Colfax. FRED PFLUGHOFT

Above: Northern fur seal. GORDON & CATHIE SULLIVAN

Right: Sunset on Ruby Beach seastacks, Olympic National Park.
FRED PFLUGHOFT

Right: Early Winter
Spires, Okanogan
National Forest.

GORDON & CATHIE SULLIVAN

Facing page: The fierce
profile of 8,840-foot
Dragontail Peak in
Alpine Lakes
Wilderness.

FRED PFLUGHOFT

Right: At Long Beach, beach grass anchors the dunes.
FRED PFLUGHOFT

Facing page: Cloud cover mimics ocean waves along the Pacific. GORDON & CATHIE SULLIVAN

Above: Southwestern Washington boasts the state's only active sandhill crane nests. GORDON & CATHIE SULLIVAN

Left: Moss-covered maples of the Hoh Rain Forest. FRED PFLUGHOFT

Facing page: The crystal-clear Skagit River in Ross Lake National Recreation Area. FRED PFLUGHOFT

Right: Icicle Creek trickles through its namesake canyon during icicle season. FRED PFLUGHOFT

Far right: A new day for Little Annapurna Peak and the Enchantment Lakes Basin in the Cascade Mountains.

FRED PFLUGHOFT

Above: Puget Sound Naval Shipyard, Bremerton. FRED PFLUGHOFT

Facing page: Seagulls pause in Rosario Strait at Deception Pass State Park, Whidbey Island. FRED PFLUGHOFT

Above: Palouse Falls' 200-foot drop is the centerpiece of Palouse State Park. FRED PFLUGHOFT

Facing page: American Ridge, Olympic National Park. GORDON & CATHIE SULLIVAN

Above: Dogwood announces spring in the Columbia River Gorge Scenic Area. FRED PFLUGHOFT

Facing page: The popular Mukilteo Ferry approaches Mukilteo Lighthouse and its museum. FRED PFLUGHOFT

Glacier Peak from Sahale Mountain in the North Cascades. FRED PFLUGHOFT

Above: Fox Cove, Sucia Island State Park in the San Juans. FRED PFLUGHOFT

Right: The Fred Redman Memorial Bridge near Yakima. FRED PFLUGHOFT

Left: In Ross Lake National Recreation Area, Colonial Peak and Pyramid Peak rise above Diablo Lake.

FRED PFLUGHOFT

Facing page: Looking west to the North Cascades.

GORDON & CATHIE SULLIVAN

Above: Makah Indian fishing canoes are designed for stability amid coastal waves.
GORDON & CATHIE SULLIVAN

Left: Along Olympic National Park's trail to Soleduck Falls. FRED PFLUGHOFT

Following pages: Ruby Beach bids another day adieu. FRED PFLUGHOFT

Above: American bittern, a heron. GORDON & CATHIE SULLIVAN

Left: Lower Granite Lake on the Snake River near Clarkston. FRED PFLUGHOFT

Above: Vine maple flashes its autumn glory. FRED PFLUGHOFT

Left: The changing season creeps up Mount Rainier.

GORDON & CATHIE SULLIVAN

Above: Lake Crescent, Olympic National Park. FRED PFLUGHOFT

Facing page: Soleduck Falls. FRED PFLUGHOFT

Above: Emmons Glacier atop Mount Rainier, tinted by the rising sun. FRED PFLUGHOFT

Facing page: Cape Horn in the Columbia River Gorge National Scenic Area. GORDON & CATHIE SULLIVAN

Above: Along Cascade River Road, Mount Baker. FRED PFLUGHOFT

Facing page: The Skagit River. GORDON & CATHIE SULLIVAN

Fred Pflughoft

Fred Pflughoft turned from watercolor painting to landscape photography in 1988. His full-color photography appears regularly in regional and national periodicals, on calendars and postcards from American and Canadian publishers, and is featured in the Farcountry Press books *Wyoming Wild and Beautiful*, *Oregon Wild and Beautiful*, *Yellowstone Wild and Beautiful*, *Grand Teton Wild and Beautiful*, *Wyoming Impressions*, and *Wyoming's Historic Forts*. He and his wife, Sue, have twin sons who join them in outdoor activities all year around.

Gordon and Cathie Sullivan

Gordon and Cathie Sullivan are full-time professional photographers who specialize in natural images of diverse geographic forms. For over twenty-five years, Gordon has honed his skills as a wilderness enthusiast and conservationist through his career in outdoor photography. In addition to her landscape photography, Cathie is accomplished in portrait work. Jointly, their dedication to wilderness and spirit shapes the Washington images collected in this volume.